Make&Take™

EASY RECIPES FOR POTLUCKS, PARTIES + PICNICS

Crowd-Pleasing
HOT DISHES

Flavor-Packed
Sandwiches & Stromboli

Easy-to-Tote
CAKES, PIES, & BARS

<<< **TOTE A SALAD IN A JAR**
1 Recipe, 40 Different Possibilities

Make&Take™

CONTENTS

CASSEROLES

Hot dishes with rich flavors and creamy goodness that will draw a crowd.

LAYERED POTATO
TACO CASSEROLE,
PAGE 3

Zucchini-Noodle Lasagna

PREP **15 minutes** BROIL **12 minutes**
BAKE **30 minutes at 375°F**
STAND **10 minutes**

- 2 lb. zucchini
  Nonstick cooking spray
- 1 lb. extra-lean ground beef
- 2 cups chopped fresh portobello mushrooms
- 2 cloves garlic, minced
- 1 24- to 26-oz. jar chunky-style pasta sauce
- 1 8-oz. can tomato sauce
- 1 tsp. dried basil, crushed
- 1 tsp. dried oregano, crushed
- 1 tsp. fennel seeds, crushed
- 1 egg, lightly beaten
- 1 15-oz. carton fat-free ricotta cheese
- 1½ cups shredded part-skim mozzarella cheese (6 oz.)
- ½ cup grated Parmesan Cheese

1. Preheat broiler. Trim ends from zucchini; cut zucchini lengthwise into ¼-inch slices. Lightly coat both sides of zucchini slices with cooking spray. Place slices, half at a time, in a single layer on a wire rack set on a large baking sheet. Broil about 6 inches from the heat for 12 to 14 minutes or until lightly browned, turning once halfway through broiling. Reduce oven temperature to 375°F.
2. For meat sauce, in a large skillet cook ground beef, mushrooms, and garlic over medium-high heat until meat is browned. Remove from heat. Stir in pasta sauce, tomato sauce, basil, oregano, and fennel seeds. In a bowl combine egg and ricotta cheese.
3. To assemble, spread 1 cup meat sauce in a 13×9-inch baking pan. Top with enough zucchini slices to cover bottom of pan. Gently spread half the ricotta mixture over zucchini; sprinkle with ¾ cup of the mozzarella cheese. Top with half the remaining meat sauce. Repeat layers starting with zucchini and ending with meat sauce.
4. Bake 20 minutes. Sprinkle with the ½ cup Parmesan cheese. Bake 10 to 15 minutes more or until cheese is melted. Let stand 10 minutes before serving. Makes 12 servings.
PER SERVING *190 cal., 7 g fat (3 g sat. fat), 59 mg chol., 575 mg sodium, 14 g carb., 3 g fiber, 19 g pro.*

ZUCCHINI-NOODLE LASAGNA

Layered Potato Taco Casserole

(*Pictured on page 1.*)
PREP 30 minutes
BAKE 1 hour 25 minutes at 350°F

　　Nonstick cooking spray
1　lb. extra-lean ground beef
1½　cups chopped green sweet peppers
1　cup chopped onion
1　14.5-oz. can diced tomatoes and green chiles, drained
1　1.25-oz. envelope lower-sodium taco seasoning mix
4　cloves garlic, minced
⅓　cup light butter with canola oil
⅓　cup all-purpose flour
¼　tsp. salt
2¼　cups fat-free milk
6　cups thinly sliced Yukon gold potatoes
1½　cups shredded reduced-fat cheddar cheese (6 oz.)
　　Light sour cream
　　Chopped tomatoes
　　Snipped fresh cilantro

1. Preheat oven to 350°F. Lightly coat a 13×9-inch baking pan with cooking spray.
2. In a large skillet cook ground beef, sweet peppers, and onion over medium heat until meat is browned. Stir in canned tomatoes, taco seasoning mix, and garlic.
3. For sauce, in a medium saucepan melt butter over medium heat. Stir in flour and salt. Gradually stir in milk. Cook and stir until thickened and bubbly. Cook and stir 1 minute more.
4. Spread half the potatoes in the prepared baking dish. Top with half the meat mixture. Drizzle with half the sauce; sprinkle with half the cheese. Repeat layers.
5. Bake, covered, 1 hour and 20 minutes. Sprinkle with remaining cheese. Bake, uncovered, 5 to 10 minutes more or until heated through. Top servings with sour cream, fresh tomatoes, and cilantro. Makes 8 servings.
PER SERVING　*341 cal., 12 g fat (6 g sat. fat), 58 mg chol., 808 mg sodium, 35 g carb., 4 g fiber, 24 g pro.*

UPSIDE-DOWN PIZZA CASSEROLE

Upside-Down Pizza Casserole

PREP 20 minutes
BAKE 15 minutes at 400°F

1½　lb. bulk Italian sausage or lean ground beef
1½　cups sliced fresh mushrooms (4 oz.)
1　15-oz. can tomato sauce with basil, garlic, and oregano
¼　cup sliced pitted ripe olives (optional)
1　to 1½ cups shredded mozzarella cheese or Italian cheese blend (4 to 6 oz.)
1　13.8-oz. pkg. refrigerated pizza crust
　　Milk
　　Grated Parmesan cheese
　　Thinly sliced pepperoni, chopped sweet pepper and/or tomatoes, sliced olives and/or fresh mushrooms, and/or fresh basil (optional)

1. Preheat oven to 400°F. In a large skillet cook sausage and mushrooms over medium-high heat until meat is browned. Drain off fat. Stir in tomato sauce and, if desired, olives; heat through. Spread in a 2-qt. rectangular baking dish. Sprinkle with mozzarella cheese.
2. Arrange pizza crust on hot beef mixture. Fold under excess crust and press along edges of dish to seal. Cut several 1-inch slits in crust. Brush with milk and sprinkle with Parmesan cheese.
3. Bake 15 to 18 minutes or until crust is lightly browned. If desired, add toppings and sprinkle with additional Parmesan cheese. Makes 6 servings.
PER SERVING　*428 cal., 22 g fat (9 g sat. fat), 84 mg chol., 1,036 mg sodium, 27 g carb., 2 g fiber, 32 g pro.*

Creamy Hot Chicken Salad

PREP 25 minutes
BAKE 25 minutes at 400°F

- ¾ cup coarsely crushed potato chips
- ½ cup chopped pecans
- 6 cups chopped cooked chicken
- 2 cups shredded cheddar cheese (8 oz.)
- 2 cups chopped celery
- 1 cup chopped red and/or yellow sweet pepper
- ¼ cup sliced green onions
- 1 10.75-oz. can condensed cream of chicken soup
- 1 cup mayonnaise
- 1 8-oz. carton sour cream
- 1 tsp. dried thyme or basil, crushed
- ¼ tsp. black pepper
  Sourdough bread slices, toasted (optional)
  Coarsely crushed potato chips (optional)
- 1 recipe Caramelized Red Onion (optional)

1. Preheat oven to 400°F. For topping, in a bowl combine ¾ cup crushed potato chips and pecans.
2. In a bowl stir together chicken, cheese, celery, sweet pepper, and green onions. In another bowl combine soup, mayonnaise, sour cream, thyme, and black pepper. Pour soup mixture over chicken mixture; fold gently to combine. Transfer to a 13×9-inch baking dish. Sprinkle with potato chip-pecan topping.
3. Bake, uncovered, 25 to 30 minutes or until heated through and bubbly around edges. If desired, serve on toasted bread and top with additional crushed potato chips and Caramelized Red Onion. Makes 12 servings.

CREAMY HOT CHICKEN SALAD

SMOKY WILD RICE CASSEROLE

PER SERVING *478 cal., 37 g fat (12 g sat. fat), 100 mg chol., 554 mg sodium, 8 g carb., 1 g fiber, 27 g pro.*
Caramelized Red Onion In a medium skillet heat 1 Tbsp. olive oil over medium heat. Add half a medium red onion, thinly sliced. Reduce heat to medium-low. Cook 8 to 10 minutes or until onion is golden, stirring occasionally.

Smoky Wild Rice Casserole

PREP 30 minutes
BAKE 20 minutes at 350°F

- 1 6-oz. pkg. or two 4.3-oz. pkg. long grain and wild rice mix
- 1 medium fennel bulb
- 1 13-oz. pkg. smoked turkey sausage, chopped
- 2 medium carrots, cut into thin strips
- ½ cup chopped onion
- 3 cloves garlic, minced
- ¼ cup all-purpose flour
- ¼ cup light sour cream
- 2 Tbsp. Dijon mustard
- 3 cups fat-free milk
- 12 oz. fresh asparagus, trimmed and cut into 2-inch lengths

1. Preheat oven to 350°F. Prepare long grain and wild rice mix according to package directions.
2. Meanwhile, trim fennel, reserving some of the feathery leaves. Cut bulb into thin slivers. In an extra-large skillet cook fennel slivers, sausage, carrots, and onion over medium heat 5 to 10 minutes or until sausage is browned and vegetables are crisp-tender, stirring occasionally. Stir in garlic.
3. In a medium bowl combine flour, sour cream, and mustard; gradually stir in milk. Add milk mixture all at once to sausage mixture. Cook and stir over medium heat until slightly thickened and bubbly. Stir in asparagus and cooked rice. Transfer to a 2½- to 3-qt. casserole.
4. Bake, covered, 20 to 25 minutes or until heated through. Top with reserved fennel leaves. Makes 6 servings.
PER SERVING *303 cal., 7 g fat (2 g sat. fat), 38 mg chol., 1,111 mg sodium, 44 g carb., 4 g fiber, 19 g pro.*

Honey-Chile Chicken on Coconut Rice

PREP 20 minutes
BAKE 45 minutes at 350°F

Nonstick cooking spray
2 cups water
1 14-oz. can unsweetened light coconut milk
1¼ cups uncooked jasmine rice
½ tsp. salt
2 tsp. olive oil
¾ cup chopped onion
¾ cup chopped yellow or red sweet pepper
2 tsp. grated fresh ginger
2 cloves garlic, minced
1½ cups frozen peas
2 Tbsp. honey
2 Tbsp. Asian chili paste (sambal oelek)
1 Tbsp. lime juice
2 tsp. reduced-sodium soy sauce
3 cups chopped cooked chicken breast
Raw chip coconut, toasted (optional)
¼ cup snipped fresh cilantro
Lime wedges and/or Asian chili paste (sambal oelek)

1. Preheat oven to 350°F. Coat a 13×9-inch baking dish with cooking spray. In a small saucepan bring the water and coconut milk to boiling; pour into the prepared baking dish. Stir in rice and salt. Bake, covered, 30 minutes.
2. Meanwhile, in a large nonstick skillet heat oil over medium heat. Add onion and sweet pepper; cook 5 minutes or just until tender, stirring occasionally. Add ginger and garlic; cook and stir 1 minute more. Stir onion mixture and peas into partially cooked rice.
3. In a medium bowl combine honey, 2 Tbsp. chili paste, lime juice, and soy sauce. Add chicken; stir to coat. Spoon over rice mixture.
4. Bake, covered, 15 to 20 minutes more or until heated through and rice is tender. Sprinkle with coconut, if desired, and cilantro. Serve with lime wedges and/or additional chili paste. Makes 8 servings.

PER SERVING 283 cal., 6 g fat (3 g sat. fat), 45 mg chol., 369 mg sodium, 36 g carb., 2 g fiber, 21 g pro.

HONEY-CHILE CHICKEN
ON COCONUT RICE

CAPRESE CASSEROLE

CHICKEN ENCHILADA PASTA

Chicken Enchilada Pasta

PREP 40 minutes
BAKE 35 minutes at 350°F

- 1 12-oz. pkg. dried jumbo shell macaroni
- 3¾ cups chopped green and/or red sweet peppers
- 1½ cups chopped red onions
- 1 fresh jalapeño,* seeded and chopped
- 2 Tbsp. vegetable oil
- 2 cups chopped cooked chicken
- 2 10-oz. cans enchilada sauce
- 1 16-oz. can refried beans
- ½ 1.25-oz. envelope taco seasoning mix (3 Tbsp.)
- ¼ tsp. salt
- 2 cups shredded Mexican four-cheese blend (8 oz.)
- 1 cup sliced green onions
- 2 cups nacho-flavor tortilla chips, crushed
  Sour cream and/or guacamole

1. Preheat oven to 350°F. Cook pasta according to package directions; drain. Rinse with cold water; drain again.

2. Meanwhile, in a large skillet cook sweet peppers, red onions, and jalapeño in hot oil over medium heat 5 minutes or until tender, stirring occasionally. Stir in chicken, ½ cup of the enchilada sauce, the refried beans, taco seasoning mix, and salt. Cook 5 minutes. Stir in ½ cup of the cheese and ½ cup of the green onions.

3. Spread 1 cup of the remaining enchilada sauce in a 13×9-inch baking dish. Spoon chicken filling into cooked shells. Arrange filled shells in the baking dish. Drizzle with remaining enchilada sauce.

4. Bake, covered, 30 minutes. Sprinkle with remaining cheese. Bake, uncovered, 5 minutes or until cheese is melted. Sprinkle with tortilla chips and remaining green onions. Serve with sour cream and/or guacamole. Makes 8 servings.

*Tip Chili peppers contain oils that can irritate your skin and eyes. Wear plastic or rubber gloves when working with them.

PER SERVING *520 cal., 20 g fat (8 g sat. fat), 56 mg chol., 1,338 mg sodium, 60 g carb., 6 g fiber, 27 g pro.*

Caprese Casserole

PREP 35 minutes
BAKE 35 minutes at 375°F

- 1 12- to 14-oz. pkg. dried whole grain medium shell pasta
- 1 Tbsp. olive oil
- 6 Tbsp. thinly sliced shallots
- 4 cloves garlic, thinly sliced
- 8 cups lightly packed fresh baby spinach or torn Swiss chard leaves
- 2 cups cherry or grape tomatoes, halved
- 1 15-oz. can reduced-sodium garbanzo beans (chickpeas) or Great Northern beans, rinsed and drained
- ¾ cup thinly sliced fresh basil
- ½ cup pitted kalamata olives, sliced
- 2 cups bottled roasted red sweet peppers, drained
- ½ tsp. salt
- 2 cups shredded mozzarella cheese (8 oz.)
- ¾ cup balsamic vinegar

1. Preheat oven to 375°F. Lightly grease a 13×9-inch baking pan; set aside. Cook pasta according to package directions. Drain pasta, reserving ¾ cup of the cooking water.

2. In a large skillet heat oil over medium heat. Add shallots and garlic; cook 3 to 5 minutes or until tender, stirring occasionally. Add spinach; cook and stir about 1 minute or just until spinach is wilted. Transfer to an extra-large bowl. Add pasta, 1½ cups of the tomatoes, the beans, ½ cup of the basil, and the olives.

3. In a blender or food processor combine roasted peppers, salt, and the reserved pasta cooking water. Cover and blend or process until smooth. Stir into pasta mixture. Transfer to prepared baking dish.

4. Bake, covered, 25 minutes; sprinkle with cheese. Bake, uncovered, 10 minutes more or until heated through and cheese is melted.

5. Meanwhile, in a small saucepan bring vinegar to boiling over medium heat; reduce heat. Boil gently, uncovered, 5 to 10 minutes or until vinegar is reduced to ⅓ cup.

6. Before serving, sprinkle pasta mixture with remaining ½ cup tomatoes and remaining ¼ cup basil. Drizzle with reduced vinegar. Makes 8 servings.

PER SERVING *355 cal., 9 g fat (3 g sat. fat), 18 mg chol., 706 mg sodium, 52 g carb., 9 g fiber, 17 g pro.*

Mushroom and Kale Casserole

PREP **40 minutes**
BAKE **40 minutes at 375°F**
STAND **15 minutes**

    Nonstick cooking spray
  8 oz. dried mafalda, pasta
    broken into bite-size pieces, or
    campanelle pasta
  2 tsp. olive oil
  ¾ cup chopped onion
  3 cups sliced fresh cremini
    mushrooms (8 oz.)
  2 cloves garlic, minced
  6 cups Tuscan kale leaves, coarsely
    chopped, or baby spinach
  1 23.8-oz. jar light pasta sauce
 1½ cups reduced-fat shredded Italian
    cheese blend (6 oz.)
  1 8-oz. can no-salt-added tomato
    sauce
  ¾ cup light ricotta cheese
  1 Tbsp. milk
  1 tsp. lemon zest
  ½ tsp. dried Italian seasoning,
    crushed
  ⅛ tsp. black pepper

1. Preheat oven to 375°F. Coat a 2-qt. rectangular baking dish with cooking spray; set aside. In a 4-qt. Dutch oven cook pasta according to package directions; drain. Return to Dutch oven.

2. Meanwhile, in a large nonstick skillet heat 1 tsp. of the oil over medium heat. Add onion; cook 3 minutes, stirring

MUSHROOM AND KALE CASSEROLE

occasionally. Add mushrooms; cook 6 minutes or until mushrooms are tender and starting to brown, stirring occasionally. Add garlic; cook and stir 1 minute more. Add to Dutch oven.

3. Wipe out skillet. Add the remaining 1 tsp. oil to skillet; heat over medium heat. Gradually add kale, tossing with tongs and cooking 6 to 8 minutes or until kale is wilted and tender (if using spinach, cook and toss 1 to 2 minutes or until wilted). Add kale to pasta mixture. Stir in pasta sauce, 1 cup of the Italian cheese blend, and the tomato sauce. Transfer to prepared baking dish.

4. In a bowl combine ricotta cheese, milk, lemon zest, Italian seasoning, and pepper. Spoon in small mounds onto pasta mixture. Loosely cover dish with foil.

5. Bake 35 minutes. Sprinkle with remaining ½ cup Italian cheese blend. Bake, loosely covered, 5 minutes more or until heated through. Let stand, covered, 15 minutes before serving. Makes 6 servings.

PER SERVING *383 cal., 9 g fat (4 g sat. fat), 23 mg chol., 588 mg sodium, 55 g carb., 7 g fiber, 22 g pro.*

Za'atar Rice-Stuffed Peppers

PREP 30 minutes
BAKE 30 minutes at 400°F

- 1 Tbsp. olive oil
- ¾ cup chopped onion
- 1 Tbsp. za'atar*
- 2 cloves garlic, minced
- ¼ tsp. crushed red pepper
- ⅛ tsp. salt
- ⅛ tsp. black pepper
- 1 15-oz. can garbanzo beans (chickpeas), rinsed and drained
- 1 15-oz. can tomato puree
- 3 cups cooked basmati rice
- 4 red and/or yellow sweet peppers
- ½ cup water
  Za'atar, chopped cucumber, and/or snipped fresh Italian parsley (optional)
- 1 5.3-oz. carton plain fat-free Greek yogurt
  Lemon wedges (optional)

1. Preheat oven to 400°F. In a large skillet heat oil over medium heat. Add onion; cook 5 minutes or until tender, stirring occasionally. Add za'atar, garlic, crushed red pepper, salt, and black pepper. Cook and stir 1 minute more. Stir in beans and tomato puree; heat through. Stir in rice.
2. Cut sweet peppers in half lengthwise. Remove and discard seeds and membranes. Divide filling among pepper halves. Place stuffed peppers in a 13×9-inch baking dish. Pour the water into dish around peppers.
3. Bake, covered, 30 minutes or until peppers are crisp-tender. If desired, top with additional za'atar, cucumber, and/or parsley. Serve with yogurt and, if desired, lemon wedges. Makes 8 servings.

*Za'atar is a mixture of sumac, sesame seeds, and herbs, such as thyme and oregano, and often salt. It is a popular spice blend throughout the Middle East.
PER SERVING *192 cal., 3 g fat (0 g sat. fat), 0 mg chol., 331 mg sodium, 36 g carb., 4 g fiber, 8 g pro.*

Za'atar Chicken and Rice-Stuffed Peppers Prepare as directed, except stir in 1½ cups chopped cooked chicken with the rice.

Polenta Bake with Summer Vegetables

PREP 35 minutes
BAKE 20 minutes at 350°F

- 1 recipe Polenta
- 1 Tbsp. olive oil
- 1 medium red sweet pepper, seeded and cut into bite-size strips
- ¾ cup chopped onion
- 2 medium zucchini, halved lengthwise and sliced ½ inch thick
- 1 cup fresh corn kernels
- 2 cloves garlic, minced
- 1 tsp. smoked paprika
- ¼ tsp. salt
- ¼ tsp. black pepper
- 2 cups cherry or grape tomatoes, halved
- 1 tsp. snipped fresh thyme
- 1 cup crumbled goat cheese (chèvre) (4 oz.)
  Snipped fresh thyme (optional)

1. Preheat oven to 350°F. Spread Polenta in a 13×9-inch baking dish.
2. Meanwhile, in a large nonstick skillet heat oil over medium heat. Add sweet pepper and onion; cook 3 minutes or until tender, stirring occasionally. Add zucchini, corn, garlic, paprika, salt, and black pepper. Cook 6 to 8 minutes or just until zucchini is tender, stirring occasionally. Remove from heat; stir in tomatoes and 1 tsp. thyme. Spoon over Polenta. Sprinkle with goat cheese.
3. Bake 20 to 25 minutes or until heated through and cheese is melted. If desired, sprinkle with additional thyme. Makes 8 servings.
Polenta In a medium saucepan bring 3 cups water to boiling. In a bowl stir together 1½ cups yellow cornmeal, 1½ cups cold water, and 1 tsp. salt; slowly add to boiling water, stirring constantly. Cook and stir until polenta returns to boiling. Reduce heat to low. Cook 10 to 15 minutes or until very thick, stirring frequently. Stir in 1 Tbsp. butter and 2 tsp. snipped fresh thyme.
PER SERVING *221 cal., 8 g fat (4 g sat. fat), 15 mg chol., 450 mg sodium, 30 g carb., 3 g fiber, 7 g pro.*

POLENTA BAKE WITH SUMMER VEGETABLES

ZA'ATAR RICE-STUFFED PEPPERS

SALADS & SLAWS

Pasta, veggies, or fresh greens—these dishes boast intriguing textures and flavors.

BAVARIAN-STYLE
POTATO SALAD,
PAGE 18

Beet, Fennel, and Apple Slaw

START TO FINISH 25 minutes

- 3 Tbsp. olive oil
- 3 Tbsp. white balsamic vinegar or white wine vinegar
- 3 Tbsp. orange juice
- 2 cloves garlic, minced
- ¼ tsp. salt
- 2 oranges, peeled and cut into segments
- 1 medium red beet, trimmed, halved lengthwise, cored, and cut into matchsticks
- 1 medium apple, cored and sliced
- 1 fennel bulb, trimmed, halved lengthwise, cored, and cut into matchsticks
- 1 small jicama, peeled and cut into matchsticks
- ½ cup firmly packed chopped fresh Italian parsley

1. For vinaigrette, in a screw-top jar combine oil, vinegar, orange juice, garlic, and salt. Cover and shake well. For slaw, in a bowl toss together the remaining ingredients. Add vinaigrette; gently toss to coat. Makes 8 servings.
PER SERVING *114 cal., 5 g fat (1 g sat. fat), 0 mg chol., 100 mg sodium, 17 g carb., 4 g fiber, 1 g pro.*

BEET, FENNEL, AND APPLE SLAW

Nuts and Berries Winter Slaw

PREP 30 minutes CHILL 1 hour

- 1 navel orange
- 3 Tbsp. packed brown sugar
- ½ tsp. kosher salt
- ½ clove garlic, crushed
- ⅛ tsp. curry powder
- ⅛ tsp. cracked black pepper
- ½ cup fresh cranberries
- 3 Tbsp. coarsely chopped red onion
- 1 Tbsp. honey
- 2 tsp. canola oil
- ¾ lb. Brussels sprouts, trimmed and very thinly sliced, or purchased shaved Brussels sprouts (about 3 cups)
- 3 Tbsp. toasted hazelnuts, coarsely chopped

1. For dressing, with a vegetable peeler, remove a wide 2-inch-long strip of peel from the orange. Peel and segment orange; set aside. In a food processor combine orange peel strip, brown sugar, salt, garlic, curry powder, and pepper. Pulse until peel is finely chopped. Add cranberries and onion; pulse until cranberries are chopped. Add orange segments and pulse to chop. Transfer to a bowl; stir in honey and oil. (Dressing can be covered and chilled up to 24 hours.)
2. In a bowl combine Brussels sprouts and dressing. Cover and chill 1 to 24 hours before serving. To serve, stir and sprinkle with hazelnuts. Makes 10 servings.
PER SERVING *62 cal., 2 g fat (0 g sat. fat), 0 mg chol., 107 mg sodium, 10 g carb., 2 g fiber, 1 g pro.*

NUTS AND BERRIES WINTER SLAW

Salad in a Jar

Grab a 2-quart jar and fill it with layers of your favorite pasta salad ingredients. Put the lid on and go! It will be the talk of the table.

2 cups packed greens
- spinach
- mixed baby lettuces
- torn romaine
- Bibb or butterhead lettuce
- arugula

⅔ cup nuts
- chopped walnuts
- chopped pecans
- chopped almonds
- pistachio nuts
- chopped hazelnuts

⅔ cup cheese
- crumbled feta cheese
- crumbled blue cheese
- shredded cheddar cheese
- diced Swiss cheese

⅔ cup dried fruits
- cranberries
- chopped apricots
- cherries
- raisins
- chopped figs

1½ cups protein
- cooked chicken breast
- cooked turkey breast
- cooked ham
- cooked pork tenderloin
- cooked beef steak
- cooked tuna
- garbanzo beans (chickpeas)

1⅓ cups vegetables
- diced red onion
- sliced celery
- chopped sweet pepper
- small broccoli florets
- thinly sliced carrots
- sliced fresh mushrooms
- halved grape tomatoes
- halved snow peas

½ cup bottled salad dressing
- champagne vinaigrette
- poppy seed dressing
- ranch dressing
- Italian dressing

1⅓ cups cooked pasta
- shells
- mini bow ties
- elbow macaroni
- rotini

SWEET AND TANGY
FOUR-BEAN SALAD

Creamy Brussels Sprouts-Bacon Salad
PREP 20 minutes CHILL 2 hours

- 1 cup mayonnaise
- ½ cup dried cranberries or cherries
- ¼ cup finely chopped red onion
- 3 Tbsp. sugar
- 2 Tbsp. cider vinegar
- 7 cups shredded Brussels sprouts
- 8 slices bacon, crisp-cooked, drained, and crumbled
- ½ cup toasted slivered almonds

1. In a large bowl combine mayonnaise, dried cranberries, onion, sugar, and vinegar. Add Brussels sprouts; stir to coat. Cover and chill 2 to 24 hours. Before serving, stir in bacon and almonds. Makes 12 servings.
PER SERVING *227 cal., 18 g fat (3 g sat. fat), 13 mg chol., 219 mg sodium, 13 g carb., 3 g fiber, 5 g pro.*

CREAMY BRUSSELS
SPROUTS-BACON SALAD

Sweet and Tangy Four-Bean Salad
PREP 30 minutes CHILL 4 hours

- 8 oz. fresh green beans, trimmed and cut into 1-inch pieces
- 1 12-oz. pkg. frozen shelled edamame
- ¾ cup cider vinegar
- ⅔ cup tomato juice
- ½ cup sugar
- ¼ cup vegetable oil
- 3 Tbsp. dry red wine or apple juice
- 2 tsp. Worcestershire sauce
- 2 tsp. Dijon mustard
- 1 clove garlic, minced
- 2 cups coarsely shredded carrots
- 1 15-oz. can red kidney beans, rinsed and drained
- 1 14.5-oz. can cut wax beans, rinsed and drained
- ½ cup finely chopped green onions

1. In a large saucepan cook green beans in boiling, lightly salted water 4 minutes. Stir in edamame. Cook 3 to 4 minutes more or just until tender; drain. Rinse with cold water; drain again.
2. In an extra-large bowl combine vinegar, tomato juice, sugar, oil, wine, Worcestershire sauce, mustard, and garlic. Stir in green beans and edamame,* carrots, canned beans, and green onions. Cover and chill 4 to 48 hours. Makes 18 servings.
* For bright color green beans, cook as directed but cover and chill them separately. Toss into salad just before serving.
PER SERVING *58 cal., 1 g fat (0 g sat. fat), 0 mg chol, 100 mg sodium, 9 g carb., 3 g fiber, 4 g pro.*

Beet Pasta Salad

PREP 30 minutes
ROAST 30 minutes at 425°F
CHILL 2 hours

 2 medium red beets, peeled and cut
    into 1-inch pieces
½ cup olive oil
 8 oz. dried medium whole grain
    shell macaroni
⅓ cup white balsamic vinegar
 1 Tbsp. snipped fresh thyme
 4 cloves garlic, minced
 1 tsp. Dijon mustard
½ tsp. salt
¼ tsp. black pepper
1½ cups red and/or yellow cherry or
    grape tomatoes, halved
¾ cup julienne carrots
½ cup thinly sliced green onions
½ cup thinly sliced celery
 1 cup crumbled blue cheese (4 oz.)
¼ cup snipped fresh Italian parsley

1. Preheat oven to 425°F. In a 2-qt.
square baking dish combine beets
and 1 Tbsp. of the oil. Roast, covered,
20 minutes. Roast, uncovered, 10 to
15 minutes more or until tender; cool.
Cover and chill 2 to 24 hours.

2. Meanwhile, cook pasta according to
package directions; drain. Rinse with
cold water; drain again.

3. In a large bowl whisk together the
remaining oil, vinegar, thyme, garlic,
mustard, salt, and pepper. Stir in pasta,
tomatoes, carrots, green onions, and
celery. Cover and chill 2 to 24 hours.
Stir in beets, cheese, and parsley before
serving. Makes 8 servings.
PER SERVING *315 cal., 19 g fat (5 g sat.
fat), 11 mg chol., 394 mg sodium, 31 g
carb., 5 g fiber, 8 g pro.*

Penne and Asparagus Salad

PREP **30 minutes** CHILL **2 hours**

- 16 oz. dried penne pasta
- 1 lb. asparagus spears, trimmed and cut into 1½-inch pieces
- 1 cup chopped red sweet pepper
- 1 cup halved, pitted kalamata olives
- 6 oz. capocollo or prosciutto, thinly sliced and coarsely chopped
- 6 oz. fontina cheese, cut into ¼-inch cubes
- 4 oz. sharp cheddar cheese, cut into ¼-inch cubes
- 4 oz. Gouda cheese, cut into ¼-inch cubes
- 1½ cups creamy garlic or creamy Italian salad dressing
- ½ cup coarsely snipped fresh basil

1. In a large Dutch oven cook pasta according to package directions, adding asparagus the last 2 minutes of cooking; drain. Rinse with cold water; drain again. Transfer to an extra-large bowl.

2. Stir in sweet pepper, olives, capocollo, fontina cheese, cheddar cheese, and Gouda cheese. Add dressing, stirring to coat. Cover and chill 2 to 24 hours. Stir in basil before serving. Makes 20 servings.

PER SERVING *263 cal., 15 g fat (5 g sat. fat), 22 mg chol., 581 mg sodium, 20 g carb., 1 g fiber, 10 g pro.*

PENNE AND ASPARAGUS SALAD

Italian Pesto Pasta Salad

START TO FINISH 30 minutes

- 8 oz. dried elbow macaroni
- 1 7- to 8-oz. jar basil pesto
- ¼ cup red wine vinegar
- ½ tsp. kosher salt
- 2 15-oz. cans cannellini beans (white kidney beans), rinsed and drained
- ½ 5-oz. pkg. baby arugula
- ½ cup shaved Parmigiano-Reggiano cheese (2 oz.)
- ¼ cup toasted pine nuts

1. Cook macaroni according to package directions; drain. Rinse with cold water; drain again.
2. In a large bowl stir together pesto, vinegar, and salt. Add macaroni, beans, arugula, half the cheese, and half the nuts; toss to combine. Serve at once or cover and chill up to 6 hours. Top with remaining cheese and nuts before serving. Makes 10 servings.

PER SERVING *244 cal., 12 g fat (3 g sat. fat), 5 mg chol., 474 mg sodium, 25 g carb., 3 g fiber, 9 g pro.*

ORZO AND OLIVE SALAD WITH SPICED CITRUS VINAIGRETTE

Orzo and Olive Salad with Spiced Citrus Vinaigrette

PREP 35 minutes CHILL 2 hours

- 1½ cups dried whole wheat or regular orzo pasta
- ½ cup orange juice
- ¼ cup snipped fresh mint
- ¼ cup lemon juice
- 2 Tbsp. honey
- 1 Tbsp. olive oil
- 1 tsp. ground coriander
- 1 tsp. grated fresh ginger
- ½ tsp. salt
- ¼ tsp. ground turmeric
- ¼ tsp. crushed red pepper
- 2 cups lightly packed fresh arugula
- 1 cup julienne carrots
- ¾ cup thinly sliced green onions
- ½ cup pitted green olives, halved
- ½ cup golden raisins

1. Cook orzo according to package directions; drain. Rinse with cold water; drain again.
2. Meanwhile, in a large bowl whisk together orange juice, mint, lemon juice, honey, oil, coriander, ginger, salt, turmeric, and crushed red pepper. Stir in orzo, arugula, carrots, green onions, olives, and raisins. Cover and chill 2 to 24 hours. Makes 8 servings.

PER SERVING *206 cal., 3 g fat (0 g sat. fat), 0 mg chol., 304 mg sodium, 40 g carb., 7 g fiber, 5 g pro.*

Deviled Egg Macaroni Pasta Salad

START TO FINISH 30 minutes

- ½ cup thinly sliced red onion
- ¼ cup cider vinegar
- 1 tsp. sugar
- 8 oz. dried elbow macaroni
- 12 hard-cooked eggs
- ½ cup mayonnaise
- 3 Tbsp. country Dijon mustard
- 1 Tbsp. water
- ½ tsp. salt
- ½ tsp. smoked paprika
- ¼ tsp. cracked black pepper
- 1½ cups very thinly sliced celery
- ½ cup chopped sweet pickles
  Smoked paprika and/or cracked black pepper (optional)

1. In a small saucepan combine onion, vinegar, and sugar. Bring to simmering, stirring occasionally. Remove from heat.
2. Cook macaroni according to package directions; drain. Rinse with cold water; drain again.
3. Meanwhile, coarsely chop one of the eggs. Halve the remaining eggs; separate yolks from whites. Coarsely chop egg whites.
4. For dressing, place yolks in a medium bowl; mash with a fork. Stir in vinegar mixture, mayonnaise, mustard, the water, salt, smoked paprika, and pepper.
5. In a large bowl combine macaroni, the reserved egg whites, celery, and pickles. Add dressing; toss gently to coat. Top with the reserved egg; sprinkle with additional paprika and/or pepper. Serve at once or cover and chill up to 6 hours. If the salad seems dry after chilling, stir in a little milk. Makes 10 servings.
PER SERVING *273 cal., 15 g fat (3 g sat. fat), 228 mg chol., 422 mg sodium, 21 g carb., 1 g fiber, 11 g pro.*

DEVILED EGG MACARONI PASTA SALAD

Peanutty Noodle Slaw

PREP 25 minutes
CHILL 30 minutes

- ¾ cup bottled Asian ginger sesame salad dressing
- 2 Tbsp. creamy peanut butter
- 6 cups shredded coleslaw mix or shredded broccoli slaw mix
- ⅓ to ½ cup thinly sliced green onions
- 2 Tbsp. toasted sesame seeds
- 1 3-oz. pkg. chicken-flavor ramen noodles (save seasoning packet for another use)
- ½ cup chopped peanuts

1. For dressing, in a screw-top jar combine Asian dressing and peanut butter. Cover and shake well, adding 1 to 2 tablespoons water if necessary to reach desired consistency.
2. In a large bowl combine coleslaw mix, green onions, and sesame seeds. Break noodles into small pieces and add to slaw. Drizzle with dressing; toss gently to coat. Cover and chill 30 minutes to 2 hours. Sprinkle with peanuts. Makes 8 servings.
PER SERVING *218 cal., 14 g fat (3 g sat. fat), 0 mg chol., 345 mg sodium, 18 g carb., 3 g fiber, 6 g pro.*

Southwestern Chicken and Macaroni Salad

PREP 35 minutes ROAST 20 minutes at 450°F STAND 15 minutes

- 2 fresh poblano chile peppers, halved lengthwise and seeded (tip, page 6)
- 1 25-oz. pkg. frozen cooked crispy chicken strips
- 8 oz. dried elbow macaroni
- ½ 8-oz. pkg. cream cheese, softened
- ¾ cup salsa
- 1 avocado, halved, seeded, peeled, and chopped

1. Preheat oven to 450°F. Line a baking sheet with foil. Place peppers, cut sides down, on the prepared baking sheet. Roast 20 minutes or until peppers are charred and very tender. Bring foil up around peppers and fold edges together to enclose. Let stand 15 minutes or until cool enough to handle. Peel off and discard skins; chop peppers.
2. Meanwhile, cook chicken and macaroni separately according to package directions. Drain macaroni; rinse with cold water and drain again. Cut chicken into ½-inch pieces.
3. In a large mixing bowl beat cream cheese and half the salsa on low until smooth. Gradually beat in the remaining salsa. Stir in roasted peppers and macaroni. Gently fold in chicken and avocado. Serve at once or cover and chill up to 2 hours. Makes 10 servings.
PER SERVING *312 cal., 14 g fat (4 g sat. fat), 37 mg chol., 600 mg sodium, 30 g carb., 3 g fiber, 17 g pro.*

Tex-Mex Potato Salad

PREP 40 minutes CHILL 6 hours

- 2 lbs. red and/or yellow new potatoes, quartered
- ¼ tsp. salt
- ¾ cup mayonnaise or salad dressing
- ¾ cup bottled ranch salad dressing
- 1 canned chipotle chile pepper in adobo sauce, finely chopped
- ½ tsp. salt
- 1 cup thinly sliced celery
- ⅓ cup chopped onion
- 6 hard-cooked eggs, coarsely chopped
- 1 cup canned black beans, rinsed and drained
- 1 cup frozen corn, thawed Tortilla chips

1. In a covered large saucepan cook potatoes with ¼ tsp. salt in enough boiling water to cover for 15 minutes or just until potatoes are tender; drain. Cool slightly.
2. Meanwhile, for dressing, in an extra-large bowl combine mayonnaise, ranch dressing, chipotle pepper, and ½ tsp. salt. Stir in celery and onion. Add potatoes, eggs, black beans, and corn; stir gently to coat. Cover and chill 6 to 24 hours. Top with tortilla chips. Makes 12 servings.

PER SERVING *300 cal., 21 g fat (4 g sat. fat), 104 mg chol., 536 mg sodium, 22 g carb., 3 g fiber, 7 g pro.*

Bavarian-Style Potato Salad

PREP 20 minutes
COOK 20 minutes

- 1½ lbs. Yukon Gold potatoes, well scrubbed
- ¼ cup white wine vinegar
- ¾ tsp. kosher salt
- ½ tsp. black pepper
- 4 slices bacon, cut into ¼-inch pieces
- ½ cup chopped red onion
- ¼ cup chicken broth
- 2 Tbsp. vegetable oil
- 1 tsp. sugar
- ¾ tsp. dried dill
- ½ tsp. celery seeds
- 2 Tbsp. snipped fresh dill or fresh Italian parsley

1. In a large saucepan cover potatoes in lightly salted water. Bring to boil. Reduce heat and simmer, covered, 20 to 25 minutes or just until tender; drain well. Rinse with cold water; cool slightly. Halve and cut potatoes into ¼-inch slices; place in a large bowl. Drizzle warm potatoes with vinegar and season with the salt and pepper.
2. For dressing, in a large skillet cook bacon over medium heat until crisp. Remove skillet from heat. Add onion, broth, oil, sugar, dill, and celery seeds to bacon and drippings; stir well to combine. Pour dressing over potatoes; gently toss to coat. Sprinkle with fresh dill. Serve at room temperature or chilled. Makes 6 servings.

PER SERVING *248 cal., 16 g fat (4 g sat. fat), 17 mg chol., 513 mg sodium, 20 g carb., 3 g fiber, 5 g pro.*

BAVARIAN-STYLE POTATO SALAD

SANDWICHES & STROMBOLI

Flavor-packed and hand-held muffulettas, subs, stromboli, and slab pies are picnic hits.

DELI-STYLE
SUBMARINES,
PAGE 21

Tote-and-Slice Loaf Sandwich

START TO FINISH **25 minutes**

- ¾ cup dried tomatoes (not oil-pack)
- 1 lb. Italian or French bread
- ½ 8-oz. pkg. cream cheese, softened
- ⅓ cup basil pesto
- 4 oz. thinly sliced provolone cheese
- 8 oz. thinly sliced pepper or regular salami
- 1 fresh banana pepper or 8 bottled banana peppers, stemmed, seeded, and sliced
- ½ red onion, thinly sliced
  Small salad peppers and/or pimiento-stuffed green olives (optional)

1. Place tomatoes in a small bowl. Add enough boiling water to cover and let stand 10 minutes. Drain tomatoes and place in a food processor; cover and process until finely chopped.

2. Split loaf in half horizontally. Hollow out the bottom half, leaving a ½-inch-thick shell.

3. Spread cream cheese on cut sides of bread halves. Spread top half with dried tomatoes and bottom half with pesto. On the bottom half, layer provolone cheese, salami, banana pepper, and onion. Place loaf top, spread side down.

4. Tightly wrap loaf with plastic wrap. To serve, slice loaf crosswise into six sandwiches. If desired, spear salad peppers and/or olives with long toothpicks; insert a toothpick through each sandwich. Makes 6 servings.

PER SERVING *588 cal., 34 g fat (14 g sat. fat), 69 mg chol., 1,645 mg sodium, 46 g carb., 4 g fiber, 24 g pro.*

NEW ORLEANS-STYLE
MUFFULETTA

Deli-Style Submarines

(Pictured on page 19.)
START TO FINISH 20 minutes

- 2 8-oz. loaves French bread
- ¾ 8-oz. carton sour cream ranch dip (12 Tbsp.)
- 1 cup torn lettuce
- ¾ cup shredded carrot
- 8 oz. thinly sliced cooked roast beef, ham, or turkey
- 1¼ cups thinly sliced cucumber
  Black pepper
- 4 oz. thinly sliced Colby Jack cheese

1. Cut bread in half horizontally. Spread cut sides of bread with dip. Layer bottom half of bread with lettuce, carrot, roast beef, cucumber, black pepper to taste, and cheese; replace top half of bread. Cut into eight portions. Makes 8 servings.

PER SERVING *283 cal., 10 g fat (6 g sat. fat), 41 mg chol., 936 mg sodium, 34 g carb., 2 g fiber, 15 g pro.*

New Orleans-Style Muffuletta

PREP 20 minutes CHILL 4 hours

- ½ cup coarsely chopped pitted ripe olives
- ½ cup chopped pimiento-stuffed green olives
- 1 Tbsp. snipped fresh Italian parsley
- 2 tsp. lemon juice
- ½ tsp. dried oregano, crushed
- 1 Tbsp. olive oil
- 1 clove garlic, minced
- 1 16-oz. loaf ciabatta bread or French bread
- 6 lettuce leaves
- 4 oz. thinly sliced salami, pepperoni, or summer sausage
- 4 oz. thinly sliced cooked ham or turkey
- 6 oz. thinly sliced provolone, Swiss, or mozzarella cheese
- 1 to 2 medium tomatoes, thinly sliced
- ⅛ tsp. coarse ground black pepper

1. For olive relish, in a bowl combine olives, parsley, lemon juice, and oregano. Cover and chill 4 to 24 hours.
2. In a bowl stir together oil and garlic. Cut bread in half horizontally. Hollow out the inside of the top half, leaving a ¾-inch shell.
3. Brush bottom half of bread with garlic oil. Layer with lettuce, salami, ham, cheese, and tomatoes. Sprinkle tomatoes with pepper. Stir olive relish; spoon on tomatoes. Replace top half. Cut into six portions. Makes 6 servings.

PER SERVING *411 cal., 20 g fat (8 g sat. fat), 47 mg chol., 1,374 mg sodium, 39 g carb., 2 g fiber, 21 g pro.*

Chicken, Bacon, and Cheddar Submarines

PREP **25 minutes**   GRILL **12 minutes**
BAKE **15 minutes at 400°F**

- 12 oz. skinless, boneless chicken breast halves
- ¼ tsp. garlic salt
- ¼ tsp. black pepper
- 1 small red onion, cut into ½-inch slices
- 1 Tbsp. olive oil
- 9 slices bacon
- ⅓ cup mayonnaise
- 1 Tbsp. coarse ground mustard
- 2 12-inch loaves baguette-style French bread
- 8 slices cheddar cheese

1. Sprinkle chicken with garlic salt and pepper. Brush onion slices with oil.

Grill chicken and onion, covered, over medium heat 12 to 15 minutes or until chicken is done (165°F) and onion is tender and lightly charred, turning once. Remove from grill. Thinly slice chicken; separate onion into rings.
2. Meanwhile, preheat oven to 400°F. Line a 15×10×1-inch baking pan with foil. Place bacon on the prepared baking pan. Bake 15 minutes or until crisp. Drain bacon on paper towels.
3. In a bowl combine mayonnaise and mustard. Cut bread loaves in half horizontally. Hollow out the inside of each half, leaving a ¾-inch shell. Spread cut sides of bread with mayonnaise spread. Layer bottom half with chicken, onion, bacon, and cheese; replace top.
4. If desired, wrap each sandwich in foil and grill, covered, 10 minutes or until

CHICKEN, BACON, AND CHEDDAR SUBMARINES

heated through, turning every 2 minutes. Cut each sandwich into four portions. Makes 8 servings.
PER SERVING *623 cal., 25 g fat (9 g sat. fat), 67 mg chol., 1,272 mg sodium, 65 g carb., 3 g fiber, 34 g pro.*

Cuban Griller

PREP **25 minutes**   CHILL **2 hours**
GRILL **30 minutes**

- 2 Tbsp. mayonnaise
- 2 Tbsp. yellow mustard
- 1 16-oz. loaf ciabatta bread or Cuban bread
- 8 oz. thinly sliced cooked ham
- 4 oz. thinly sliced roast pork
- 4 oz. thinly sliced salami
- 10 lengthwise sandwich dill pickle slices
- 6 oz. sliced Swiss cheese
  Nonstick cooking spray

1. In a small bowl combine mayonnaise and mustard. Cut bread in half horizontally. Spread cut sides of bread with mayonnaise mixture. Layer bottom half of bread with ham, pork, and salami. Pat pickles dry with paper towels; place on meat. Add cheese. Replace top half of bread; press down firmly.
2. Coat a 24×18-inch sheet of heavy foil with cooking spray. Tightly wrap sandwich in the greased foil. Wrap in a second sheet of foil; place on a baking sheet. Place a heavy skillet on top of sandwich to press ingredients firmly together; chill 2 to 24 hours.
3. Grill sandwich, covered, over medium-low heat 30 minutes, turning every 5 minutes. Cut into eight portions. Makes 8 servings.
PER SERVING *365 cal., 17 g fat (7 g sat. fat), 63 mg chol., 1,188 mg sodium, 30 g carb., 1 g fiber, 23 g pro.*

CUBAN GRILLER

Cobb Salad Sub

PREP 30 minutes STAND 15 minutes

- 3 Tbsp. olive oil
- 1 Tbsp. white wine vinegar
- 1 tsp. Dijon mustard
- ½ tsp. freshly ground black pepper
- ¼ tsp. salt
- 2 cups cubed cooked chicken or turkey
- 1 avocado, halved, seeded, peeled, and chopped
- ⅔ cup chopped roma tomatoes
- 4 slices bacon, crisp-cooked, drained, and crumbled
- 1 1-pound loaf French bread
- 2 cups chopped bibb or Boston lettuce
- ¼ cup crumbled blue cheese (2 oz.)
- 2 hard-cooked eggs, chopped

1. For dressing, in a small bowl whisk together oil, vinegar, mustard, pepper, and salt.

2. In a bowl combine chicken, avocado, tomatoes, and bacon. Pour dressing over chicken mixture; toss to coat.

3. Cut a wedge in the top of the bread about 1 inch from edges. Use your hands to pull out some of the inside of the loaf, leaving about a ¾-inch shell. Layer in lettuce, chicken mixture, cheese, and eggs. Let stand 15 minutes before slicing with a long serrated knife. Or wrap and chill up to 2 hours. Makes 6 servings.

PER SERVING *416 cal., 20 g fat (5 g sat. fat), 113 mg chol., 675 mg sodium, 33 g carb., 3 g fiber, 25 g pro.*

COBB SALAD SUB

Spinach Fontina Stromboli

PREP 20 minutes RISE 20 minutes
BAKE 25 minutes at 375°F
STAND 10 minutes

- 2 tsp. olive oil
- 1 Tbsp. cornmeal
- 1 16-oz. loaf frozen whole wheat bread dough, thawed
- 1 cup shredded fontina cheese (4 oz.)
- 1 cup baby fresh prewashed spinach or torn spinach
- ¼ cup kalamata olives, pitted and chopped
- 1 egg, lightly beaten

1. Lightly brush a baking sheet with olive oil; sprinkle with cornmeal. On a lightly floured surface, roll bread dough into a 13×10-inch rectangle. Sprinkle with half the cheese. Layer spinach over cheese. Top with remaining cheese and olives. Roll up dough, starting from the long side. Pinch dough to seal the seam and ends, using wet fingers, if necessary.
2. Place loaf, seam side down, on prepared baking sheet. Brush with egg. Using a sharp knife, cut slits in top for steam to escape. Cover and let rise in a warm place 20 to 25 minutes. Preheat oven to 375°F. Bake 25 minutes or until golden brown. Let stand 10 minutes. Makes 4 servings.
PER SERVING 506 cal., 22 g fat (7 g sat. fat), 79 mg chol., 666 mg sodium, 61 g carb., 6 g fiber, 19 g pro.

HAM, CHEESE, AND TURKEY STROMBOLI

Ham, Cheese, and Turkey Stromboli

PREP 20 minutes
BAKE 30 minutes at 375°F

- 1 tsp. olive oil
- 1 Tbsp. cornmeal
- 1 13.8-oz. pkg. refrigerated pizza dough
- 4 oz. thinly sliced cooked ham
- 1 cup shredded mozzarella cheese (4 oz.)
- 1 cup fresh baby spinach or torn spinach leaves
- 4 oz. thinly sliced cooked turkey
- ⅓ cup chopped red, green, or yellow sweet pepper
- ¼ cup kalamata olives, pitted and chopped
- 1 egg, lightly beaten
  Marinara sauce or pizza sauce (optional)

1. Preheat oven to 375°F. Lightly brush a baking sheet with oil; sprinkle with cornmeal.
2. On a lightly floured surface, roll pizza dough into a 13×10-inch rectangle. Arrange ham slices on dough to within ½ inch of the edges. Sprinkle with ½ cup of cheese. Layer spinach and turkey on cheese. Top with the remaining ½ cup cheese, the sweet pepper, and olives. Starting from a long side, roll up dough; pinch to seal seams.
3. Place loaf, seam side down, on prepared baking sheet. Brush with egg; cut a few slits in top for steam to escape. Bake 30 minutes or until golden. Cool slightly. If desired, serve with marinara sauce. Makes 4 servings.
PER SERVING 417 cal., 17 g fat (5 g sat. fat), 93 mg chol., 1,290 mg sodium, 44 g carb., 3 g fiber, 23 g pro.

SPINACH FONTINA STROMBOLI

Ham and Cheese Slab Pies

PREP 30 minutes
BAKE 25 minutes at 400°F

- 6 oz. cream cheese, softened
- 2 Tbsp. honey mustard
- 1 17.3-oz. pkg. frozen puff pastry sheets, thawed (2 sheets)
- 6 oz. thinly sliced Black Forest ham
- ½ medium red onion, thinly sliced
- 6 oz. thinly sliced Gruyère, Swiss, or cheddar cheese
- 1 egg, lightly beaten
- 1 Tbsp. water

1. Preheat oven to 400°F. Line two large baking sheets with parchment paper. In a bowl combine cream cheese and mustard.

2. On a lightly floured surface, roll each sheet of pastry into a 15×12-inch rectangle. Transfer each rectangle to a prepared baking sheet.

3. Spread half of each pastry rectangle lengthwise with cream cheese mixture, leaving a ½-inch border around outside edges. Layer ham, onion, and sliced cheese on cream cheese layer. In a bowl combine egg and the water; brush some of the mixture over edges of pastry. Fold pastry over filling and press edges with a fork to seal. Brush tops with the remaining egg mixture; cut slits in tops to let steam escape.

4. Bake 25 minutes or until golden, covering loosely with foil if tops brown too quickly. Slide pies on parchment paper onto wire racks; cool slightly. Makes 12 servings.

PER SERVING *360 cal., 26 g fat (9 g sat. fat), 56 mg chol., 361 mg sodium, 21 g carb., 1 g fiber, 11 g pro.*

HAM AND CHEESE SLAB PIES

SWEETS

End potlucks on a sweet note with easy-to-tote cakes, bars, and rustic pies.

CHOCOLATE
PICNIC CAKE

Chocolate Picnic Cake

PREP 20 minutes
BAKE 30 minutes at 350°F

1½	cups sugar
3	Tbsp. unsweetened cocoa powder
	Dash salt
½	cup heavy cream
¼	cup milk
1	Tbsp. vanilla
1	cup chopped walnuts
1	cup semisweet chocolate pieces
½	cup sugar
2¼	cups all-purpose flour
1½	cups sugar
⅓	cup unsweetened cocoa powder
1½	tsp. baking soda
½	tsp. salt
1½	cups water or strong brewed coffee, cooled
½	cup canola oil
4½	tsp. vinegar
1½	tsp. vanilla

1. Preheat oven to 350°F. Grease and flour a 13×9-inch baking pan. For the chocolate sauce, in a heavy saucepan combine sugar, cocoa powder, and salt. Stir in heavy cream and milk. Bring to a gentle boil, stirring constantly, reduce heat. Cook and stir 2 minutes. Remove from heat; stir in vanilla. Transfer to a bowl; cover surface with plastic wrap. Cool to room temperature.
2. For the picnic topping, in a bowl combine walnuts, chocolate pieces, and sugar.
3. In a large bowl stir together flour, sugar, cocoa powder, baking soda, and salt. Stir in the water, oil, vinegar, and vanilla. Beat batter with a fork until smooth. Pour into prepared pan. Sprinkle with picnic topping.
4. Bake 30 to 40 minutes or until a wooden toothpick inserted near center comes out clean. Cool cake slightly in pan on a wire rack. Serve warm with a scoop of vanilla ice cream and drizzle with chocolate sauce. Makes 12 servings.
PER SERVING *722 cal., 32 g fat (11 g sat. fat), 46 mg chol., 334 mg sodium, 107 g carb., 4 g fiber, 8 g pro.*

CHOCOLATE-PECAN
COFFEE CAKE

Chocolate-Pecan Coffee Cake

PREP 30 minutes
BAKE 55 minutes at 325°F
COOL 20 minutes

½	cup butter, softened
1	cup granulated sugar
2	tsp. baking powder
½	tsp. baking soda
¼	tsp. salt
2	eggs
1	tsp. vanilla
2¼	cups all-purpose flour
1	8-oz. carton sour cream
1	recipe Coconut-Pecan Topping

1. Preheat oven to 325°F. Grease and flour a 10-inch fluted tube pan; set aside. In a large mixing bowl beat butter with a mixer on medium to high 30 seconds. Add the sugar, baking powder, baking soda, and salt. Beat until well combined, scraping sides of bowl occasionally. Add eggs one at a time, beating well after each addition. Beat in vanilla. Alternately add flour and sour cream to butter mixture, beating on low after each addition just until combined.
2. Sprinkle half the Coconut-Pecan Topping in the tube pan. Spoon half the cake batter in mounds over the coconut mixture. Carefully spread to an even layer. Sprinkle with remaining Coconut-Pecan Topping. Spoon on remaining cake batter and spread to an even layer.
3. Bake 55 to 65 minutes or until a long wooden skewer inserted near center comes out clean. Cool on a wire rack 20 minutes. Invert cake and remove pan. Serve warm. Makes 12 servings.
Coconut-Pecan Topping In a bowl combine 1 cup flour, 1 cup packed brown sugar, and 1 tsp. ground cinnamon. Cut in ½ cup cold butter until mixture resembles coarse crumbs; stir in ¾ cup semisweet chocolate pieces, ½ cup flaked coconut, and ½ cup chopped pecans.
PER SERVING *550 cal., 28 g fat (16 g sat. fat), 86 mg chol., 297 mg sodium, 71 g carb., 2 g fiber, 6 g pro.*

Ginger Pear Galette

PREP 25 minutes
BAKE 25 minutes at 400°F

½ 17.3-oz. pkg. frozen puff pastry
   sheets, thawed (1 sheet)
1 egg white, lightly beaten
2 Tbsp. all-purpose flour
2 Tbsp. granulated sugar
2 Tbsp. packed brown sugar
1 Tbsp. finely chopped crystallized
   ginger
1 tsp. lemon zest
2 Tbsp. butter
3 large pears, peeled and thinly
   sliced
   Whipped cream (optional)

1. Preheat oven to 400°F. Line a baking
sheet with parchment paper; set aside.
On a lightly floured surface, unfold
pastry. Roll into a 14×11-inch rectangle;
trim to a 12×10-inch rectangle. Place on
the prepared baking sheet. Brush edges
of pastry with egg white. Cut ½-inch
strips from pastry trimmings. Place
strips on edges of pastry rectangle,
pressing to form raised rim; trim ends.
Brush edges again with egg white. If
desired, decorate edges with cutouts
from pastry trimmings and brush
cutouts with egg white. Prick center of
pastry rectangle with a fork.
2. For topping, in a bowl stir together
flour, granulated sugar, brown sugar,
crystallized ginger, and lemon zest. Cut
in butter until pieces are pea size.
3. Sprinkle half the topping on pastry.
Arrange pear slices on tart, overlapping
slightly. Sprinkle with remaining topping.
4. Bake 25 minutes or until pastry is
golden and pears are tender. If desired,
top with whipped cream. Serve warm.
Makes 8 servings.
PER SERVING *282 cal., 15 g fat (5 g sat.
fat), 8 mg chol., 106 mg sodium, 36 g carb.,
3 g fiber, 3 g pro.*

EASY APPLE-
CRANBERRY
SLAB PIE

Easy Apple-Cranberry Slab Pie

PREP 25 minutes
BAKE 50 minutes at 375°F

2½ lb. cooking apples, peeled, cored,
    and thinly sliced (7 cups)
⅔ cup dried cranberries
⅔ cup granulated sugar
¼ cup all-purpose flour
½ tsp. ground cinnamon
1 17.3-oz. pkg. frozen puff pastry,
   thawed (2 sheets)
   Milk
   Coarse sugar
1 cup powdered sugar
½ tsp. vanilla
   Dash salt
4 to 5 tsp. milk

1. Preheat oven to 375°F. Lightly grease
a 15×10-inch baking pan. For filling,
stir together apples, dried cranberries,
granulated sugar, flour, and cinnamon.
2. On a lightly floured surface, unfold
one sheet of pastry. Roll into a
15×10-inch rectangle. Transfer to the
prepared baking pan. Spread filling in
pastry to within 1 inch of edges.
3. Unfold the remaining sheet of pastry;
roll into a 16×11-inch rectangle. Place
on filling. Moisten edges of bottom
pastry with milk. Fold bottom pastry
over top pastry; gently press edges to
seal. Using a sharp knife, cut slits in
pastry. Brush lightly with milk and
sprinkle with coarse sugar.
4. Bake 50 to 55 minutes or until
filling is bubbly and pastry is puffed
and golden. If needed to prevent
overbrowning, cover pie loosely with
foil the last 10 to 15 minutes of baking.
5. For icing, stir together powdered
sugar, vanilla, and salt. Stir in enough
milk to reach drizzling consistency.
Drizzle icing over warm pie. Cool on a
wire rack. Makes 12 servings.
PER SERVING *346 cal., 13 g fat (0 g sat.
fat), 0 g chol., 168 mg sodium, 57 g carb.,
3 g fiber, 2 g pro.*

GINGER PEAR GALETTE

Berry-Rhubarb Bars
PREP 30 minutes
BAKE 1 hour 5 minutes at 350°F
CHILL 2 hours

    Nonstick cooking spray
3 cups quick-cooking rolled oats
2 cups all-purpose flour
1½ cups sugar
1½ cups butter
4 cups chopped fresh or frozen rhubarb
⅔ cup sugar
½ cup water
1 tsp. ground ginger
4 cups fresh raspberries
    Vanilla ice cream (optional)
    Fresh raspberries (optional)

1. Preheat oven to 350°F. Line a 13×9-inch baking pan with foil, extending foil over edges of pan. Coat foil with cooking spray.
2. In a large bowl stir together oats, flour, and 1½ cups sugar. Using a pastry blender, cut in butter until mixture resembles coarse crumbs (use fingers, if necessary, to break up mixture). Remove 3 cups for topping. Press the remaining oat mixture onto bottom of prepared baking pan. Bake 20 minutes.
3. Meanwhile, for filling, in a large saucepan combine rhubarb, ⅓ cup sugar, the water, and ginger. Bring to boiling, stirring to dissolve sugar. Reduce heat. Cook, uncovered, over medium heat 5 to 7 minutes until liquid is syrupy. Remove from heat. Stir in raspberries. Carefully spoon filling over hot baked crust. Sprinkle with reserved oat mixture.
4. Bake 45 minutes or until top is golden and filling is bubbly. Cool in pan on a wire rack. Chill 2 to 24 hours before serving. Using edges of foil, lift uncut bars out of pan. Cut into bars. If desired, serve with ice cream and fresh berries. Makes 32 servings.
PER SERVING *197 cal., 9 g fat (6 g sat. fat), 23 mg chol., 70 mg sodium, 27 g carb., 2 g fiber, 2 g pro.*

Butterscotch-Pretzel Bars

PREP 25 minutes
CHILL 2 hours

    Nonstick cooking spray
1½ cups powdered sugar
1 cup creamy peanut butter
6 Tbsp. butter, melted
2 cups crushed pretzels
1 11-oz. pkg. butterscotch-flavor pieces (2 cups)
¼ cup heavy cream
½ cup coarsely crushed pretzels
½ cup chopped peanuts

1. Line a 13×9-inch pan with foil, extending foil over edges of pan. Lightly coat foil with cooking spray; set pan aside. For crust, in a large bowl combine powdered sugar, peanut butter, and melted butter. Stir in 2 cups crushed pretzels. Press into prepared pan.
2. In a medium-size heavy saucepan stir butterscotch pieces and cream over low heat just until butterscotch pieces are melted.

3. Spread butterscotch mixture over crust. Sprinkle with ½ cup crushed pretzels and peanuts; press gently. Cover and chill at least 2 hours. Using edges of foil, lift uncut bars out of pan. Cut into bars. Makes 36 servings.
PER SERVING *166 cal., 10 g fat (5 g sat. fat), 7 mg chol., 154 mg sodium, 17 g carb., 1 g fiber, 3 g pro.*

CHEWY CHOCOLATE-CARAMEL BARS

Chewy Chocolate-Caramel Bars

PREP 25 minutes
BAKE 25 minutes at 350°F

1 pkg. 2-layer-size German chocolate cake mix
¾ cup butter, melted
1 5-oz. can evaporated milk
1 14-oz. pkg. vanilla caramels, unwrapped
1 cup chopped walnuts
1 cup semisweet chocolate pieces (6 oz.)

1. Preheat oven to 350°F. Grease a 13×9-inch baking pan; set aside. In a large mixing bowl beat cake mix, melted butter, and ⅓ cup of the evaporated milk with a mixer on medium until smooth. Spread half the dough in prepared baking pan.
2. In a large heavy saucepan stir caramels and remaining evaporated milk over medium-low heat until melted and smooth. Pour over dough in pan. Sprinkle with nuts and chocolate pieces. Crumble remaining dough over nuts and chocolate pieces.
3. Bake 25 minutes. Cool in pan on a wire rack. Cut into bars. Makes 48 servings.
PER SERVING *140 cal., 8 g fat (4 g sat. fat), 9 mg chol., 115 mg sodium, 17 g carb., 1 g fiber, 1 g pro.*

Lush Lemon Blondies

PREP 30 minutes
BAKE 30 minutes at 325°F

1½ cups all-purpose flour
1 tsp. baking powder
¼ tsp. salt
½ cup butter, softened
¾ cup packed brown sugar
½ cup granulated sugar
2 eggs
2 tsp. vanilla
½ cup toasted chopped macadamia nuts
1 10-oz. jar lemon curd

1. Preheat oven to 325°F. Line a 9-inch square baking pan with foil, extending foil over edges of pan. Grease foil.
2. In a bowl stir together flour, baking powder, and salt. In a large bowl beat butter with mixer on medium to high 30 seconds. Add sugars. Beat 5 minutes, scraping bowl occasionally. Add eggs, one at a time, beating well after each addition. Beat in vanilla. Gradually add flour mixture, beating on low until combined. Stir in ⅓ cup of the macadamia nuts.
3. Spread one-third of the batter in prepared baking pan. At 1-inch intervals drop large spoonfuls of lemon curd onto batter. Top with remaining batter. Gently swirl a knife through batter and lemon curd layers to marble. Sprinkle with remaining macadamia nuts.
4. Bake 30 minutes or until golden and set. Cool in pan on wire rack. Using edges of foil, lift cookies out of pan. Cut into bars. Makes 20 servings.
PER SERVING *240 cal., 8 g fat (4 g sat. fat), 44 mg chol., 107 mg sodium, 32 g carb., 2 g fiber, 2 g pro.*

LUSH LEMON BLONDIES

BROWNED-BUTTER BLONDIES

Browned-Butter Blondies

PREP 20 minutes
BAKE 35 minutes at 325°F

1 cup butter
2 cups all-purpose flour
1 tsp. baking powder
1 tsp. salt
¼ tsp. baking soda
1½ cups packed brown sugar
½ cup granulated sugar
2 eggs
2 tsp. vanilla
1 cup coarsely chopped toasted pecans (optional)
⅔ cup almond toffee bits (optional)
Caramel-flavor ice cream topping (optional)

1. Preheat oven to 325°F. Line a 13×9-inch baking pan with foil, extending the foil over edges of pan. Grease foil.
2. In a small saucepan melt butter over medium heat until foamy. When foaming subsides, swirl pan constantly over medium heat until butter is golden brown and fragrant. Immediately remove from heat. In a bowl stir together flour, baking powder, salt, and baking soda.
3. In a large mixing bowl combine the browned butter, brown sugar, granulated sugar, eggs, and vanilla. Beat with a mixer on medium until thick and smooth. Add flour mixture, one-third at a time, beating on low after each addition just until combined. Batter will be very thick. If desired, stir in pecans. Spread batter in prepared baking pan. If desired, sprinkle with toffee bits.
4. Bake 35 minutes or until a wooden toothpick inserted near center comes out clean. Cool in pan on a wire rack. Using edges of foil, lift uncut bars out of pan. Cut into bars. If desired, drizzle bars with caramel-flavor ice cream topping and sprinkle with additional chopped toasted pecans and almond toffee bits. Makes 32 servings.
PER SERVING *186 cal., 10 g fat (5 g sat. fat), 29 mg chol., 176 mg sodium, 23 g carb., 1 g fiber, 2 g pro.*

Peanut Butter-Jam Bars

PREP 20 minutes
BAKE 25 minutes at 375°F

- ¾ cup butter, softened
- ½ cup creamy peanut butter
- 1½ cups packed brown sugar
- 1 tsp. vanilla
- ½ tsp. baking soda
- ½ tsp. salt
- 2¼ cups quick-cooking rolled oats
- 2 cups all-purpose flour
- 1 12-oz. jar seedless blackberry, raspberry, or strawberry jam
- 1 cup chocolate-covered peanuts, coarsely chopped

1. Preheat oven to 375°F. Line a 13×9-inch baking pan with foil, extending foil over edges of pan. Lightly grease foil.

2. For crust, in a large mixing bowl beat butter and peanut butter with a mixer on medium to high 30 seconds. Add brown sugar, vanilla, baking soda, and salt. Beat until combined, scraping sides of bowl occasionally. Beat in oats. Beat in as much of the flour as you can with the mixer. Stir in any remaining flour (mixture will be crumbly). Remove 2 cups for topping. Press remaining mixture into prepared baking pan.

3. In a bowl stir jam until smooth. Carefully spread jam over crust to within 1 inch of the edges. Sprinkle with reserved oat mixture and chocolate-covered peanuts.

4. Bake 25 to 30 minutes or until jam is bubbly and topping is golden. Cool in pan on a wire rack. Using edges of foil, lift uncut bars out of pan. Cut into bars. Makes 32 servings.

PER SERVING 213 cal., 9 g fat (4 g sat. fat), 12 mg chol., 121 mg sodium, 32 g carb., 2 g fiber, 3 g pro.

Salted Chocolate Chip Cookie Sticks

PREP **35 minutes**
BAKE **22 minutes at 375°F/10 minutes at 325°F** COOL **1 hour**

- 1 cup butter, softened
- 1½ cups packed brown sugar
- ¾ tsp. salt
- ½ tsp. baking soda
- 2 eggs
- 2 tsp. vanilla
- 2¾ cups all-purpose flour
- 2 cups coarsely chopped semisweet or bittersweet chocolate
  Sea salt flakes

1. Preheat oven to 375°F. Line a 13×9-inch baking pan with foil, extending foil over edges of pan.
2. In a large bowl beat butter with a mixer on medium 30 seconds. Add brown sugar, salt, and baking soda. Beat until combined, scraping bowl as needed. Beat in eggs and vanilla. Beat in flour. Stir in chocolate. Press dough into prepared pan. If desired, sprinkle lightly with sea salt.
3. Bake 22 to 25 minutes or until light brown and center is set. Cool in pan on a wire rack 1 hour.
4. Preheat oven to 325°F. Using foil, lift cookies out of pan. Cut in half lengthwise; cut crosswise into ½- to ¾-inch-thick slices. Place, cut sides down, on an large ungreased cookie sheet. Bake 10 to 12 minutes or until cut edges are dry. Carefully remove; cool on wire racks. Makes 36 servings.
PER SERVING *166 cal., 8 g fat (5 g sat. fat), 24 mg chol., 178 mg sodium, 23 g carb., 1 g fiber, 2 g pro.*

SALTED CHOCOLATE CHIP COOKIE STICKS

Salted Almond Brownies

PREP **25 minutes**
BAKE **40 minutes at 350°F**

- 8 oz. unsweetened chocolate, coarsely chopped
- 1 cup butter
- 3 cups sugar
- 6 eggs
- 2 tsp. vanilla
- 2 cups all-purpose flour
- 2 Tbsp. unsweetened cocoa powder
- ½ tsp. baking soda
- 1 11.5-oz. pkg. milk chocolate pieces
- 1½ cups coarsely chopped smoked or regular salted almonds
- ¼ tsp. sea salt (optional)

1. In a large saucepan stir unsweetened chocolate and butter over low heat until melted and smooth. Remove from heat; cool.
Preheat oven to 350°F. Line a 13×9-inch baking pan with foil, extending foil over edges of pan. Grease foil; set aside.
2. Stir sugar into chocolate mixture. Add eggs, one at a time, beating after each addition just until combined. Stir in vanilla. In a small bowl stir together flour, cocoa powder, and baking soda; stir into chocolate mixture just until combined. Stir in 1½ cups of the milk chocolate pieces. Spread batter in prepared baking pan. Sprinkle with remaining milk chocolate pieces, almonds, and, if desired, salt.
3. Bake 40 minutes. Cool in pan on a wire rack. Using edges of foil, lift uncut brownies out of pan. Cut into bars. Makes 32 servings.
PER SERVING *299 cal., 17 g fat (9 g sat. fat), 54 mg chol., 120 mg sodium, 35 g carb., 3 g fiber, 5 g pro.*

INDEX

SALTED CHOCOLATE CHIP COOKIE STICKS